A NORMAL SKIN

A NORMAL SKIN

John Burnside

CAPE POETRY

First published 1997

1 3 5 7 9 10 8 6 4 2

© John Burnside 1997

John Burnside has asserted his right
under the Copyright, Designs and Patents Act 1988
to be identified as the author of this work

First published in the United Kingdom in 1997 by
Jonathan Cape,
Random House, 20 Vauxhall Bridge Road, London SW1V 2SA

Random House Australia (Pty) Limited
20 Alfred Street, Milsons Point, Sydney,
New South Wales 2061, Australia

Random House New Zealand Limited
18 Poland Road, Glenfield,
Auckland 10, New Zealand

Random House South Africa (Pty) Limited
Box 2263, Rosebank 2121, South Africa

Random House UK Limited Reg. No. 954009

A CIP catalogue record for this book
is available from the British Library

Papers used by Random House UK Limited are natural,
recyclable products made from wood grown in sustainable forests.
The manufacturing processes conform to the environmental
regulations of the country of origin.

ISBN 0 224 04286 6

Typeset by Palimpsest Book Production Limited,
Polmont, Stirlingshire
Printed and bound in Great Britain by
Creative Print and Design (Wales), Ebbw Vale

FOR SARAH

*When the mind is like a hall in which thought is like a voice speaking,
the voice is always that of someone else.*

Wallace Stevens

*And if the soul, too, my dear Alcibiades, is to know itself, it must surely
look into a soul.*

Plato: *Alcibiades I*

*Out of this same light, out of the central mind,
We make a dwelling in the evening air,
In which being there together is enough.*

Wallace Stevens

ACKNOWLEDGEMENTS

Acknowledgements are due to *College Green, Columbia, London Quarterly, London Review of Books, New Orleans Journal, PN Review, Poetry Postcards Quarterly, Poetry Review, Quadrant, Scotsman, The Times Literary Supplement*.

'Agoraphobia' and 'Ukiyo-e' first appeared in the *New Yorker*.

CONTENTS

A NORMAL SKIN

The wet days come like a rash:
after a month of sun, the windowpanes
are clouded with the afterlife
of cat fur and busy-lizzies,
and, gloved in her latest attack
of eczema, our silent neighbour
sits between her curtains like a burning
candle, her face turned aside,
her shoulders hunched.
She's taking apart the clocks she collected all year
at boot fairs and local fêtes
and laying them out in pieces on the table.
She knows how things are made – that's not the point –
what matters is the order she creates
and fixes in her mind:
a map of cogs and springs, laid out in rows,
invisibly numbered.
                        What we desire in pain
is order, the impression of a life
that cannot be destroyed, only dismantled.
For years you would buy those razors with orange handles,
the toothpastes and mild shampoos for a sensitive skin
I never had. For years, I took apart
the memories I thought would make me whole
being unravelled.
                        What we desire in pain
is reason: an impression of ourselves
as wounded, explained,
coerced from a destination.
                        Late at night,
our neighbour draws her curtains, disappears,
and lies in the healing darkness, half-awake,
achieving a normal skin

by an effort of will.
                    I'm not the one you thought
was sensitive, the soul you hoped to find:
arriving home, still wet with moonlit rain,
I enter the silence you left, in a dreamless house,
and reckon how little I feel,
when I stop to listen.

CHIAROSCURO

Fixing his practised gaze
on the darkest wall,

the artist unexpectedly reveals
a martyred saint.

The ribs are trodden in,
he's crowned with thorns,

and someone has thrust a lantern to his face
to offer the *coup de grâce*.

The finest glaze
is vested in this blade;

but somewhere else, behind a veil of smoke,
the kitchen girl is lit, against her will,

turning away from the gleam
of gutted fish

and letting her own knife
trickle from her hands

as if she'd just recalled
a lover's skin;

and somewhere else,
beyond the chandler's yard,

October begins in the furthest
angle of brick,

a thinning of the light,
a splash of gold,

the neighbours' orchards, moving slowly
closer, in the first grey wash of dawn.

SNAKE

As cats bring their smiling
mouse-kills and hypnotised birds,
slinking home under the light
of a summer's morning
to offer the gift of a corpse,

you carry home the snake you thought
was sunning itself on a rock
at the river's edge:
sun-fretted, gracile,
it shimmies and sways in your hands
like a muscle of light,
and you gather it up like a braid
for my admiration.

I can't shake the old wife's tale
that snakes never die,
they hang in a seamless dream
of frogskin and water,
preserving a ribbon of heat
in a bone or a vein,
a cold-blooded creature's
promise of resurrection,

and I'm amazed to see you shuffle off
the woman I've know for years,
tracing the lithe, hard body, the hinge of the jaw,
the tension where sex might be, that I always assume
is neuter, when I walk our muffled house
at nightfall, throwing switches, locking doors.

A PROCESS OF SEPARATION

The business of love is
cruelty which,
by our wills,
we transform
to live together.
(William Carlos Williams)

I ECHO PIT ROAD

All afternoon the house has filled with bees:
drifting between the mirrors, brushing the glass
with creosote, they magnetise the air
till I can feel the dead against my skin,
the standstill of accomplished memory.
At dusk I see my father in the yard:
drained of regret, in a raincoat and leather gloves,
he sets his ladder to the cherry tree
and climbs unsteadily to where
a little owl is tangled in the nets.
Now he is working slowly, to cut it free:
holding the wings in his fist while he tugs it loose,
he pitches the bird aside and turns his face,
awkward and well-intentioned, self-betrayed,
revealing the gap in his hands
to the gathering darkness.

Your sister called to talk while we were out.
I played the tape; that rancour in her voice
cut like a knife.
        No ghosts on Barton Road:
beyond the edge of town, amongst the trees
our porch light glimmers, blue as paraffin;
the deer come through at dusk; the dogs run wild;
passing foxes rummage in the bins
for pig-bones and fat.
We sit up late, inventing dialogue.
I understand too well your fear of touch,
the hunger you displace with memories,
the badger in the soul, the totem beast
that digs beneath the house, kicks up a stink,
comes to our bed in the moonlight, to plead contrition.

It's autumn all afternoon:
the light between dog and wolf,
a cold rain fuzzing the trees

on Barton Road. I'm listening;
if anything exists besides ourselves
I'll hear it on the air:

the creak of water stalling in the pipes,
a fall of soot, the first milk of decay
filming the bones of mice beneath the stairs

— a softer voice than any I'd imagine,
giving itself away
in the hush of dusk.

You won't allow cats in the house,
and even our quietest moments are immune
to badgers and hunting owls,

though somewhere along this street, a sleeping woman
drifts in a sulphurous tide of flying ants,
and lightning spirits brush the holly trees

at Gosden, where the old men lie awake,
fishing for catfish and dace
in a river of static.

So much of flesh is grass, you find yourself
in ramsons and the smell of bittercress,
in mullein and foxgloves, lighting the summer nights,

and golden iris hanging in the porch
to keep us safe. You bury stones and feathers in a jar
to drive all thought of evil from the door,

while I construct this tunnel in the dark:
cockchafers; worms; a cobweb of blood on my tongue;
and all the time I long for transformation,

subsisting in the shadow of the house:
containing, like a cyst, my father's soul,
his cryptic love, his taste for carrion.

On the way home, I hit
a rabbit or a fox-cub
in the dark.
The snapped bone echoed for miles
in the taut suspension:
ripples of tooth and nail
in the meat of my spine.
I'm frightened now:
a spirit haunts my dreams,
I wake before dawn
and her peeled face
rises to meet me.
You never see. You fade and reappear
like Lazarus:
sometimes I find bright jars
of oxblood, or flowers of sulphur,
buried in the cupboard understairs;
sometimes I find you sleeping in the day,
accepting the shape of the dead
like you want it to happen.

Lately, I feel an echo in my hands,
an awkwardness he never failed to mask,
a lack of grace. All I have learned
I want to learn again:
fumbling in the cold to tie a line;
letting the fish slide free
in the fleeting water.
This is the art of erasure, my father's craft:
working towards inevitable blanks
where children, or a woman's face had been;
recovering the forms he painted out:
a lover's shadow hidden in a vase,
a bowl of fruit, a blaze of drapery
– and memory is all accomplishment:
in every flaw, admission of desire,
the unexpected error of inclusion.

The girl I remember
is holding a jessed and hooded
falcon at the centre of her eye:
shy as a Berber, she watches as the flash-bulb
etches out this portion of her soul.

Though spirit may be all
the camera ignores
– motion and change, the simmer of recognition,
certainly, potential, self-deceit –
she can't avoid some loss of gravity.

Now she is giddy, wanting her father's hand:
his knotted bones, his pigeon-coloured veins;
now I remember nothing but the grip
of talons, and the weight I cannot lose,
the falcon turning, borrowed from the air,
my unexpected kinship with its hunger.

White ants are eating his face,
stripping the shape from the bone
in the dreaming river,
gnawing away the fingernails and hair,
devouring the scourged remains,
the crown of thorns.
Now he will rise again and wander home:
drawn from the earth, he takes on human form,
he peels me from the air, wraps me in blood,
steps into my flesh and walks away.
I know this ghost. It's only a drift of smoke
in the summer darkness,
fox-piss lining the hedges, road-kills and dew.
Something from nowhere: the wet shirt peeled from my back
on the first day of school;
the fear of manhood; cloakroom mysteries;
the pit cage where the colliers went down
to miles of gas; the silence in the barn,
that blood-warmth I couldn't explain
in the lath and plaster.
Sleeping, I meet the knacker's bloodless stare,
his salty fingers rolling back my tongue,
probing the milk-teeth,
feathering the palate.
I've watched him skin a carcass in the yard:
skilful and unrepentant, drenched in blood,
he scattered the wet remains across the earth
and entered them, becoming what he killed.
Once I reached in and touched the smoking lungs,
the barrel of the ribs, the cooling heart.
Now I go out at dawn and walk the meadows,
searching for the image of a fox,
a rat, a weasel – anything but man.

My fingers are wrapped in leaf-mould
and stagnant mud,
chained to my father, rooted in his hands,
remembering his body as he comes
through quicklime and spawn to touch me in the dream
and whisper, through the resurrected mask,
give everything you have to feed this longing.

What animals are these, come from the fields,
shifting from form to form
in our clouded garden?

I watch till they become invisible
then reappear an arm's length further on:
shy; evasive; grounded in the shadows.

What little I know of houses
I leave behind:
the stubborn light, the scents that never fade,

asparagus and old machinery
pinning your memory down
in the empty kitchen;

the brand of soap you liked, the after-shave,
folding you into the dust
of the upper rooms.

Those animals return with every flitting:
strangers arrive and find them in the porch
decaying slowly, lingering for days,

or lost between the floorboards and the wall:
a knot of hair;
an aftermath of feathers.

MUDDY ROAD BY ADAM JOHNSON'S HOUSE

after Andrew Wyeth ✗

It's this knowing the land by the names
of neighbours: the long-deceased

and the newborn:
the tactful farm-wives standing in their yards;

the hedges and orchards
grubbed out years ago,

but lit in the mind
with ghost rain fuzzing the leaves;

and, under it all, the pure geography
of childhood walks and first snow and the time

you stopped at Kuerner's barn to warm your hands
and saw a young buck pouring from the roof,

the ankles crossed, the last thick cloud of steam
hanging around the muzzle and the groin,

its dying the heat you breathed
in the first chill of winter.

✗ American
Realist painter
1917 – 2009
I enjoy his work
very much, like
I enjoy the poetry
of Robert Frost

16

LIBERTAD

Once, on a wooded hill
above Segovia,

we pulled in under some pine trees,
out of the sun,

and walked for miles
along a sandy road.

The rye-grass was spotted
with bullets – a strange red fruit –

and, halfway in,
I found what remained of a doe,

the mossed head buried in silt
and a tinder of needles.

I still recall
how quietly we stared,

bewildered and fixed by a sudden
tug of compassion

– not for the slaughtered deer,
but for ourselves:

the keys in my pocket,
our passports, your printed scarf;

the awkwardness
of wanting to go on.

THE MAN WHO WAS ANSWERED BY
HIS OWN SELF

after Tirzah Ravilious

It happens to me
in the dream:
I'm standing in this room, in black and white,

a village implied by the window – hydrangeas and light
and people walking home
from evensong.

It's summer. I'm wearing the same
striped shirt,
immersed in the man my mother would have liked:

well-groomed, well-dressed,
not too intelligent.
The phone rings and I reach to pick it up

or is it me who calls – I'm not quite sure –
but there, at the end of the line
is another voice

I know is me, my own self calling home
from somewhere different.
He's talking about a world

that might have been:
the same hydrangeas, smudged with dust and rain,
the same trees, the same wide streets,

but colour has intervened, complexity, detail,
the subtleties we miss, to manage
comfort with ourselves and one another.

Sometimes, you can look up from a book
and notice that more time has passed
than you would have expected,

the world going dark outside, the garden
dusted with soot, your fingers
stiffening, all of a sudden, becoming

no more than they seem.
It happens to me,
in the dream:

I answer the phone and the dark world is quietly
present: my own voice
lush as the midsummer distance where towns dissolve,

their people back from church, adjusting the dials
on empty wirelesses and tuning in
to nothing, to their own selves, calling home.

FIFTEEN WORDS FOR SNOW

In that last year he worked for the council
my cousin would take me out
on graveyard work,

mowing the strips of grass between the stones
or spraying the gravel paths
with the taste of diesel

he'd dole out random scraps of information,
facts about outer space, or puffer fish,
ancient cultures, murders, kangaroos,

how someone could drown in a teaspoonful of water,
and how the Inuit
have fifteen words for snow

describing a world too subtle for our eyes,
an infinite grading of white
and unwavering movement.

Later, I learned that most of what he said
was false,
and some of the time, at least,

he was having me on;
but even now, I navigate a world
he part-invented,

expecting to wake some morning, grey-haired and mad,
unable to tell
what happens in the dark,

or driving the country roads, in the gathering dusk,
expecting to meet the image of myself
who'd vanish if ever I stopped

to let him in.

SNØLØSNING

A word for the moment when trees and dry-stone walls
emerge from their huddle of snow

like new-formed beasts, still dark from the womb
that shaped them;

for the morning when you walk the road to town
and each white neighbour steps out from his lair

of tea and spirits, lingonberry jam,
fish sealed in jars, old letters, old desires,

and stands in his shirt sleeves, waiting for the light
to quicken. At times like this

you know the soul is real, a malted stain
that hangs behind a door, disguised as silk,

a woman's scarf,
a veil of nets and lines,

something a lover or friend once left behind
and promised to retrieve, next time around.

THE BLIND

On Tuesdays they walked from school
to the public baths,

passing our window, leaving us unseen
in every weather: flecked with snow or rain,

they marched in pairs, a good eight hundred yards
of guesswork.

All afternoon I pictured them
swimming in silence,

attuned to one another through the play
of water and skin,

imagining some kinship with the drowned
they might possess, unknowing: how they would guess

at motion and other lives
through the palm-smooth tiles;

and later, through trig,   *trigonometry*
I heard them walking back

and waited for the first blithe face to show
beyond the fence, the tap of whited canes

tracing a current home, through bricks and tar:
magnetic; guided; rooting in the darkness.

RESTORING INSTRUMENTS

Why they should smell
of butterscotch, or fern,

I never understand:
given the same dark wood, the same faint grain,

the innermost corners
silvered with dust and rosin.

Once a viola came. I could almost taste
the woman: Chanel No. 5;

a gust of body warmth across the bridge;
a dab of sweat.

I cradled it for hours
between my hands,

fingered the bow,
tapped softly on the strings,

imagined I heard a voice
in the bright harmonics.

FEEDING THE CLOWNFISH

The fish
are sceptical.
They've been in this world before
and know what is wanting,

and how would they avoid
desire and fear,
colliding with the mystery of glass,
the tremor of my voice, my clumsy hands,

unless they had accomplished
true detachment?
I've wondered what they think, scouting the tank;
I've watched them for a flicker of belief,

impatience, terror, consternation, joy
– and nothing shows, not even
memory.
   In all this time, I think,
they've never slept,

so never dream
– unless their dream is everything I take
for granted, too immediate to doubt:
the table in the hall; the second post;

the lights across the firth; the empty green;
homecoming children, calling in the dark;
the perfume on your headscarf
spiced with rain.

THE WOMAN TAKEN IN ADULTERY

I'm thinking of her house:

the white of her bed;
                        the sweet smell
of sage or persimmons;

the promise she keeps to herself
when she opens the door:

sunlight in the yard;
                        the sound of birds;
the salt between her fingers, when the man
slips out.

        That good hour, when she walks
from room to room,

or stands in the kitchen, naked,
                        alone for once,
lifting a pitcher of milk
                        to the bruise of her mouth.

JUDAS

The needy one
        who'd dip into your flesh
to witness love

        who
walks the garden
        coming with the dawn
to steal your dream

        who'd
bleed you dry
        then sit awake all night
weaving the jaundiced cloak
        of an affection.

SIMON OF CYRENE

Here's the definitive
                    bystander:

trapped in the smell of wood and a scrawl
of dust
            he enters what will pass
for history.

Taking the cross from the convict's
birdlike hands

he thinks of his children,
                            his wife
in her garden of vines,

then shoulders the weight.

He wasn't meant
                to get involved in this.

Like everyone
            he should be somewhere else.

VANISHING TWIN

I remember the fields of grain
in my sister's dream,
the fox on the wall of the church, the slow
pull of the river,

but how could she see, when I was suspended in gold,
an amniotic light, a steady
pulse against the newly-furnished bone?

She bled away. But sometimes I wake in the dark
and feel her with me, breathing through the sheets,
or I turn in the shimmer of day
and catch her out:

my opposite, though still identical,
she's reaching down to haul me from a web
of birthmarks, age lines, scars beneath the skin.

AGORAPHOBIA

My whole world is all you refuse:
a black light, angelic and cold,
on the path to the orchard,
fox-runs and clouded lanes and the glitter of webbing,
little owls snagged in the fruit nets
out by the wire

and the sense of another life, that persists
when I go out into the yard
and the cattle surround me, obstinate and dumb.
All afternoon, I've worked at the edge of your vision,
mending fences, marking out our bounds.
Now it is dusk, I turn back to the house

and catch you, like the pale Eurydice
of children's classics, venturing a glance
at nothing, at this washed infinity
of birchwoods and sky, and the wet streets leading away
to all you forget: the otherworld, lucid and cold

with floodlights and passing trains and the noise of traffic,
and nothing like the map you sometimes
study, for its empty bridlepaths,
its hill-tracks and lanes, and roads winding down to a coast
of narrow harbours, lit against the sea.

I've visited the place
where thought begins:
pear trees suspended in sunlight, narrow shops,
alleys to nothing

but nettles
and broken walls;
and though it might look different
to you:

a seaside town, with steep roofs
the colour of oysters,
the corner of some junkyard with its glint
of coming rain,

though someone else again would recognise
the warm barn, the smell of milk,
the wintered cattle
shifting in the dark,

it's always the same lit space,
the one good measure.
Sometimes you'll wake in a chair
as the light is fading,

or stop on the way to work
as a current of starlings
turns on itself
and settles above the green,

and because what we learn in the dark
remains all our lives,
a noise like the sea, displacing the day's
pale knowledge,

you'll come to yourself
in a glimmer of rainfall or frost,
the burnt smell of autumn,
a meeting of parallel lines,

and know you were someone else
for the longest time,
pretending you knew where you were, like a diffident tourist,
lost on the one main square, and afraid to enquire.

Puddles of *mirin* and soy
on our crusted plates,

daikon, matsuba,
a half-eaten muscle of eel,

and those plums in their bitter juice
at the rim of your bowl,

as if we had met in Kyoto
or ghostly Nagoya

and climbed here out of the snow
through a lake of bamboo.

The drum bridge at Kameido almost appears
when I open the curtains,

then drizzle, and London Road,
and the old

hospital, locked in its acre
of knotweed and pines:

those smudges of black on the leaves
like a printmaker's ink,

drying for two hundred years,
while we almost recover

the smoke of Minami,
the vinegar hidden in thaw.

A PHOTOGRAPH OF OLD WEST FIFE

I'm thinking of when you could buy
returns
            Of buses that no longer run
beyond the cemetery to glittering
alleys of beech mast and moss
                        Of towns that no longer

figure on the maps

                    Of thin men printed in coal

on a misted glass

                Of Geraldine

Cecilia
        Yvonne

            Of Gala Days

                        Of turning around
and smelling the wind off the Forth
on Stenhouse Street

                    I'm thinking of myself
of picking the leaves from a wall
of privet and tasting the sap

of wading across the burn at Fulford bridge
my sandals filling with water, my bare feet

chilled to the bone

        Of darkness and the echo in the woods
come out to touch my face and make me strange

an arm's length away from the dead
                  or a mile from home.

CHILDREN SLEDDING IN THE DARK,
MAGDALEN GREEN

We have studied the colours of night:
loan-path ambers, hedges dipped in bronze,
jade-tinted snow

and nothing is wholly true
till we believe:
the sky is glass, the distance is a train,

angels are sealed in the gaps
of walls, their fledged wings
spreading through mortar,

and under the lamps, possessed by the pull of the dark,
these children hold the glow
of the imagined,

perfect and hard, arriving at copper or gold
by guesswork; trusting what's contrived in flesh
to echo in the rooms of gravity.

*the distance is a train in the distance –
or the loneliness is a harp in the distance*

SHIOCHIE'S HILL, DUNKELD

I want to begin again,
climbing through beech roots and gulls
to the hill of the fairies,

to nest with the rooks, to sleep
amongst broken yews,
to crouch in the dark of the ice house, close to the stone;

I'll come after dark and feel the wet
drift of their bodies,
they'll share me with the foxes and the deer,

or borrow my human warmth
to weave a caul
for the child they have stolen

and though I could say they are only
imagined,
the shiver in me that puts them there is real,

a wish for something quick against a skin
that cools too soon,
and wears itself too lightly.

A NOH MASK

There's the pleasure of wearing a mask
in childhood:
of holding your breath
and thinking you've really changed,
becoming a smoother skin, a harder stare,

or peeling away the face you wear for others
and finding a darker child
at the back of your mind,
two parts pretence, though still
all tooth and claw.

A chance to suffer, too; to be the freak.
For moments at a time I could become
one of those babies they showed at the county fair,
sealed in its jar like a plum, forever
hanging, in a smoke of formalin.

But this is different: the mask
another face that's waited in the flesh
to be expressed:
as if I'd promised, all along, to match
the white of your Shakumi with my bronzed

Shikami – not a real pretence at all,
only the game we've played
a hundred times:
echo and answer, memory and fear,
negotiated space, between the smiles.

AT MONIACK MHOR

Miles from home
I open an upstairs window

and listen:
it's only the wind, of course, but I thought your voice

had blown through the common gold
of gorse and broom,

and later, as the farmyards still
and darken

the gap between one bird call
and the next

is almost the silence I hear
when you raise your arms

and gather the mass of your hair
for the lamplit glass.

FÉLICITÉ ET PERPÉTUÉ

Now that we have found
our dwelling place,

a patio, a shed,
a patch of green,

the gardens I intended to create
still haunt me, on those winter afternoons

when new frost powders the walls
and the empty beds:

climbing roses, snowdrops, apple trees,
the conifers and herbs I know by heart,

ghostings of *Gloire de Versailles*
on the summer air,

the soft fall of Worcester Pearmain
on fretted grass;

mornings I would wander through the wild
enclosure, where the night had slithered in,

blue stains under the lime trees, feathered kills,
the orchard sprouting mistletoe and faint

traces of angel, hanging in the boughs
like lanternlight;

the pond I would have edged
with irises, then filled with mirrored fish,

to go out, year on year,
and watch them spawn:

the butt and glide of carp
amongst the weeds,

muscles of koi
suspended in the dawn.

ANSTRUTHER

Watching the haar move in
I think of the times we came out here, as children,

and disappeared like ghosts
into the fog:

ghosts for ourselves, at least; we were still
involved with substance

and swallows flickering along the rim
of light and sand

avoided us, no matter how we tried
to be invisible.

The far shore, that I used to think
was somewhere strange,

the lighthouse that once seemed large
and fishing boats beneath the harbour wall

are forming anew
within this fold of mist,

more real than ever, harder and more precise,
and nothing ghostly in the way

the cold welds to my skin
and lets me know

how quick I am, how quick I have to be
to go on walking, blindly, into silence.

FLOATING

I love this: how you weave our journey home
through narrow streets and hushed, expectant lanes,

as if you would have us lost, amidst the blur
of bricks and glass.

It's late July: the elms are shot with light;
the sycamores are glazed with honeydew.

We park above the town
and climb the hill:

the houses here are floating in the last
glimmer of day

and further up the street, beyond the church,
a woman is leaning out from an upper room

and singing along with the music that plays
behind her

          — If not for you — babe / couldn't find
                         the door - DYAN

She's pleased with herself and sharing
more than the song with anyone who stops

to listen
        and we wait to hear it out,
the man's voice under the woman's like a slowed

current, and the words a brief accord
between them: balanced; floating in the blue.

EPITHALAMIUM

Da kam ich auf einen breiten Weg;
da kam ein Engelein und wollt' mich abweisen.
Ach nein! Ich ließ mich nicht abweisen!

(Des Knaben Wunderhorn)

I SHEKINAH

I've heard how the trawlermen harvest
quivering, sexless fish
from the ache of the sea;
how they stand on the lighted decks and hold
the clouded bodies,
watching the absence form in those buttoned eyes
and thinking of their children, home in bed,
their songless wives, made strange by years of dreaming.
I've heard that seal-folk drift in from the haar
through open doors,
the cold that strokes your lips while I am gone,
probing your sleep and stealing a little warmth
to mimic love
— so, driving back, it's always a surprise
that coming home is only to the given:
old gardens in Lochgelly, thick with privet;
still-pools of oil and silt at Pittenweem;
lights on the Isle of May; the low woods
filling with salted rain beyond Markinch.
It's always a surprise: the stink of neeps;
the malt-spills of autumn fields, where floodlit tractors
labour and churn;
the last few miles of wind and scudding clouds,
or starlit silence, hung around the house,

44

as vivid as the angel who attends
all marriages.
                    Its shimmer on our bed
is subtle, but it keeps us to itself,
learning the make-believe of granted love,
and this is all we know, an angel's gift:
that weddings are imagined, love's contrived
while each of us has one more tale to tell,
the way you feel the turning of the tide
beneath the house, or somewhere in the roof,
or how I sometimes linger on the stairs,
listening for nothing, unconvinced,
less husband than accomplice to the dark,
beguiled by the pull of the moon
and the leylines of herring.

Remembering the story of a man
who left the village one bright afternoon,
wandering out in his shirt-sleeves and never returning,
I walk in this blur of heat to the harbour wall,
and sit with my hands in my pockets, gazing back
at painted houses, shopfronts, narrow roofs,
people about their business, neighbours, tourists,
the gaunt men loading boats with lobster creels,
women in hats and coats, despite the sun,
walking to church and gossip.
It seems too small, too thoroughly contained,
the quiet affliction of home and its small adjustments,
dogs in the backstreets, barking at every noise,
tidy gardens, crammed with bedding plants.
I turn to the grey of the sea and the further shore:
the thought of distance, endless navigation,
and wonder where he went, that quiet husband,
leaving his keys, his money,
his snow-blind life. It's strange how the ones who vanish
seem weightless and clean, as if they have stepped away
to the near-angelic.
The clock strikes four. On the sea wall, the boys from
    the village
are stripped to the waist and plunging in random pairs
to the glass-smooth water;
they drop feet first, or curl their small, hard bodies to a ball
and disappear for minutes in the blue.
It's hard not to think this moment is all they desire,
the best ones stay down longest, till their friends
grow anxious, then they re-emerge
like cormorants, some yards from where they dived,
renewing their pact with the air, then swimming back
to start again. It's endlessly repeatable, their private game,

exclusive, pointless, wholly improvised.
I watch them for a while, then turn for home,
made tentative, half-waiting for the day
I lock my door for good, and leave behind
the smell of fish and grain, your silent fear,
our difficult and unrelenting love.

The wind has sealed our house with a thin
layer of dust;
study the landing windows and you'll find
tiny particles of leaf and shell,
insect bodies, crystals of salt and mica.
The radio's playing; you've put the kettle on
and, standing in your winter coat and gloves,
you listen to that song you've always liked,
the one about love.
Somewhere outside, in the gradually stilling world,
a bus has stalled, the driver
turning the engine, over and over again,
and someone's dog is barking at the noise,
guarding its phantom realm of bricks and weeds.
All over Fife, the roads
are blocked with fallen trees and stranded cars,
the tide keeps washing wreckage to the shore,
splints of timber, fishnets, broken toys.
This wind has blown for days across the fields,
so now the silence feels unnatural,
as if the storm is what we really need,
the sound of it, its small, forensic pleasures,
ribbons of silt or birchseed in the hall,
a feather on the bedroom windowsill,
and what we might discover of ourselves
and one another, as the night begins.
So much that moves around us in the dark
is ours: the smallest shiver in the hedge
a knowledge we have waited years to learn,
and something come inside, in that one
moment, when you hold the door ajar,
more than a gust of rain, more than the wind,
more than the Halloween ghosts we might imagine.

Those animals that figure on the walls,
those creatures we imagine on the stairs
are real, and we must give them shapes and names,
feed them with blood and salt, fix them a bed,
make shift, make good, allow them this possession.

IV BORDERS

A mile inland, foxes begin.
We see them working the fields
like patient farmers,
hunting for rabbits and voles
behind the dunes,
aware of us as strange, peripheral,
almost unreal:
                        By now we belong
to the sea,
to lights on the firth and the sifting
of water and sand.
Our dreams are all of fish we cannot name,
slivers of ice or metal in the nets,
mackerel shedding their scales and becoming
children, like the creatures who appear
when we sprinkle a handful of salt
on a dying fire,
figments of longing,
ghosts from the shriven past.
A mile inland, the guard-dogs and wintered cattle
know nothing of tides;
people go out at dawn, to taste the earth
that clings to their walls and their houses,
pinning them to transience and loss,
gaps in the kirkyard, the lifelong remoteness of stars.
Out here, it seems
the harbour never changes:
cormorants; gulls; the same boats moored by the wall,
Gemini, Sapphire, Reaper, Lucky Strike.
Nothing's impermanent here, where nothing
is ever untouched by the wind, or the salted rain;
though our dreams can recur for weeks, they will still remain
unknowable, repeated in the dark

as everything's repeated: love; regret;
the lights across the water, drawing in
like friendly animals we might have known
from somewhere else, some childhood we have lost
and turn to one another to renew
with questions, dares, evasions, hunted looks.

We have to drive the length of Fife to work,
moving from sunlight to frost, from brightness to fog,
each fence post and wind-thrawn tree
familiar as a road-sign
or a steeple.
This is the journey we'll make
all winter,
snow on the roofs, the street trees dusted with salt
like Nativity angels;
the land around us silent as a trap;
roads washed with light, peewits and crows in the fields,
the schoolhouse clock suspended in mid-air,
white-faced, exact,
like something achieved,
then forgotten.
This is the winter we'll learn
again and again,
like alchemy, not turning lead to gold, but finding
ways to persist, to go on for no good reason,
choosing our landmarks, finding the best way home.
Meanwhile, the road is clear: the gardens and hedges
glitter with dew;
yewberries melt and leave their fleshly stains
on cinder paths and flagstones in the park;
and here, in the lane, behind the Catholic church,
a litter of small, gold apples, newly-fallen,
wet with thawglass
after last night's frost
— crab-apples, worthless and bright
in the morning sun,
like something that might have been left behind
to signal a transmutation.
We'll spend a lifetime

finding useless gold,
and learning how to read it as a sign:
the angel we've imagined in our path,
a stain on the daylight, as close as I am to you,
closer by far, and far more dangerous.

The light is angelic and black,
the waves lap the harbour wall
like a form of laughter,
salt-laughter, drawn from the depths,
like the names of fishes.
At night, on the swaying deck, in the singing wind,
the trawlerman will find himself alone,
forgetting his thoughts, aware of the moving dark,
and listening to something he can hear,
he knows must be imagined.
                   When he turns
to call out to his neighbour, no one's there;
but something he saw through the rain, a face, a wing,
will haunt him for years,
the way it shone like home,
so far at sea.
Yet home belongs at sea: that tang of salt,
that smell of flesh and rain
                        – what little we know
of houses, we have learned
from sirens: how to walk our new-made lawns,
singing the names of flowers like a spell
to make them true,
cornflower, lily, sea-holly, rhododendron,
roses for scent and colour, yew for its fruits,
tubers and pistils, seed-pods and sacs of nectar.
What little we know of houses, we achieve
against the wind, the motion of the tides,
the pebbles and pockmarked stones we bring indoors
at random, for no good reason, and perhaps
against our wills.
The day is angelic; black; but we have fashioned
circles of grey against the coming light,

and sit at home, pretending to be safe,
aware of the siren calling in the bay,
the voice that only enters through the gaps
we leave in this invention of a life,
but enters still, to part us from ourselves
and one another: creatures from the sea
who know how long before the tide returns.

I want to plant the garden with forsythia;
not for its busy flowers, the strident
yellows fading to clusters
of watered cream,
and not for the coarse-haired leaves
that follow, like a clumsy afterthought;
it's just that I'd have a sign
to augur spring,
to come in from the garden, where I've stood
hanging the wash, or watching the sky for rain
and tell you:
the forsythia's in bloom.
I want to plant the beds with chionodoxa,
narcissus poeticus, iris reticulata,
lacecap hydrangeas, peonies, meconopsis,
so nothing will be missed: the smallest change,
blossom-break, first-fruit, leaf-fall,
coming snow.
I want to know when every lily blooms,
to read our garden like a favourite book
and find you, as you step in from the heat,
clouded with pollen, scented with grain and sap;
to know you as the locals know
the names of fields and long-abandoned wells,
gossip from way back,
the best place for sloes, or apples.
I want to step out at night, when you're asleep
and sit beside the pool, watching the fish:
stars on the water, the orange carp hanging in pairs
as if they meant to mirror one another,
making a game of likeness, matching
shadow with shadow; the patterns of colour and scale
echoed in the water as they glide,

so separate, so bright within their world,
plugged into one tight current of tension and sound,
and only a notion of difference by which
to flicker apart, and tell themselves
one from another.

As morning moves in from the firth
I'm sitting up awake, a mug of tea
fogging the window, the bones of my hands and face
shot with insomnia's delicate, lukewarm needles.
You're still asleep. Your hair is the colour of whey
and your hand on the pillow is clenched, like a baby's fist
on a figment of heat, or whatever you've clutched in a dream,
and I suddenly want to ask
your forgiveness, for something deliberately
cruel in the way I see, in the way
all seeing could become: too hard, too clear,
refusing to find something more than the cool of morning.
It's Halloween; if only because the dead
will come all afternoon to walk the streets
in faded hats and 1950s coats,
or gather by the harbour after dark
watching for lights beyond the lights we know,
their eyes like the eyes of seals, their faces
meltwater blue, as if they had surfaced through ice,
I want to go outside and gather
buckets of rain-washed apples, scabs of leaf,
a handful of broken coal, or a yellowed stump
of spindlewood, to feed the kitchen fire,
then watch, as it dwindles to ash
by late afternoon;
or wander all day in the kirkyard, reading the names
on strangers' graves: their plots laid side by side
with those they loved and hated, those they feared;
friends who betrayed them; children who watched them die.
It's what they meant by coming to this place
and choosing to remain, though decades fastened their hands
to kindling and wire, and the dampness that seeped through
     the walls

all winter long.
       Now, suddenly, you're talking in your sleep,
your face on the pillow like one of those paper masks
we used to make in school, for Halloween,
talking to someone you've dreamed, while your white hands
fasten on something fragile or easily lost,
a strand of hair, a ring, a stranger's arm,
the promise you have to remember, that brings us home.

PENITENCE

I was driving into the wind
on a northern road,
the redwoods swaying around me like a black
ocean.
    I'd drifted off: I didn't see the deer
till it bounced away,
the back legs swinging outwards as I braked
and swerved into the tinder
of the verge.
    Soon as I stopped
the headlamps filled with moths
and something beyond the trees was tuning in,
a hard attention
boring through my flesh
to stroke the bone.
    That shudder took so long
to end, I thought the animal had slipped
beneath the wheels, and lay there
quivering.
    I left the engine running; stepped outside;
away, at the edge of the light, a body
shifted amongst the leaves
and I wanted to go, to help, to make it well,
but every step I took
pushed it away.
    Or – no; that's not the truth,
or all the truth:
now I admit my own fear held me back,
not fear of the dark, or that presence
bending the trees;
not even fear, exactly, but the dread
of touching, of colliding with that pain.
I stood there, in the river of the wind,

for minutes; then I walked back to the car
and drove away.
                        I want to think that deer
survived; or, if it died,
it slipped into the blackness unawares.
But now and then I drive out to the woods
and park the car: the headlamps fill with moths;
the woods tune in; I listen to the night
and hear an echo, fading through the trees,
my own flesh in the body of the deer
still resonant, remembered through the fender.